GRAPHIC LIBRARY™

INVENTIONS AND DISCOVERY

Hedy Lamarr
AND A SECRET COMMUNICATION SYSTEM

by Trina Robbins

illustrated by Cynthia Martin
and Anne Timmons

Consultants:

Jill S. Tietjen
Professional Engineer
President and CEO
Technically Speaking, Inc.

A... ...ia
Profess... ...ngineer
Bureau of La... Management

Capstone
press®

Mankato, Minnesota

Graphic Library is published by Capstone Press,
1710 Roe Crest Drive, North Mankato, Minnesota 56003.
www.capstonepub.com

Library of Congress Cataloging-in-Publication Data
Robbins, Trina.
    Hedy Lamarr and a secret communication system / by Trina Robbins; illustrated by Cynthia
Martin and Anne Timmons.
    p. cm.—(Graphic library. Inventions and discovery)
    Includes bibliographical references and index.
    ISBN-13: 978-0-7368-6479-4 (hardcover)
    ISBN-10: 0-7368-6479-2 (hardcover)
    ISBN-13: 978-0-7368-9641-2 (softcover pbk.)
    ISBN-10: 0-7368-9641-4 (softcover pbk.)
    1. Spread spectrum communications—Juvenile literature. 2. Lamarr, Hedy, 1915– —Juvenile
literature. 3. Motion picture actors and actresses—United States—Biography—Juvenile literature.
I. Martin, Cynthia. II. Timmons, Anne. III. Title. IV. Series.
TK5103.45.R63 2007
621.384092—dc22   2006004104

Summary: In graphic novel format, tells the story of how Hollywood star Hedy Lamarr came up
with the idea for a secret communication system, which would much later become the basis for
wireless technology.

Designer
Alison Thiele

Editor
Tom Adamson

Capstone Press thanks Hedy's son, Anthony Loder, for his kind help in preparing this book.

Editor's note: Direct quotations from primary sources are indicated by a yellow background.

Direct quotations appear on the following pages:
Page 12, quoted in "Popping Questions at Hedy Lamarr" by Helen Hover (*Motion Picture*,
    March 1945).
Pages 20, 25, 27, quoted in an e-mail message from Anthony Loder to the author (May 2005).

Printed and bound in the USA.
112018 000056

TABLE OF CONTENTS

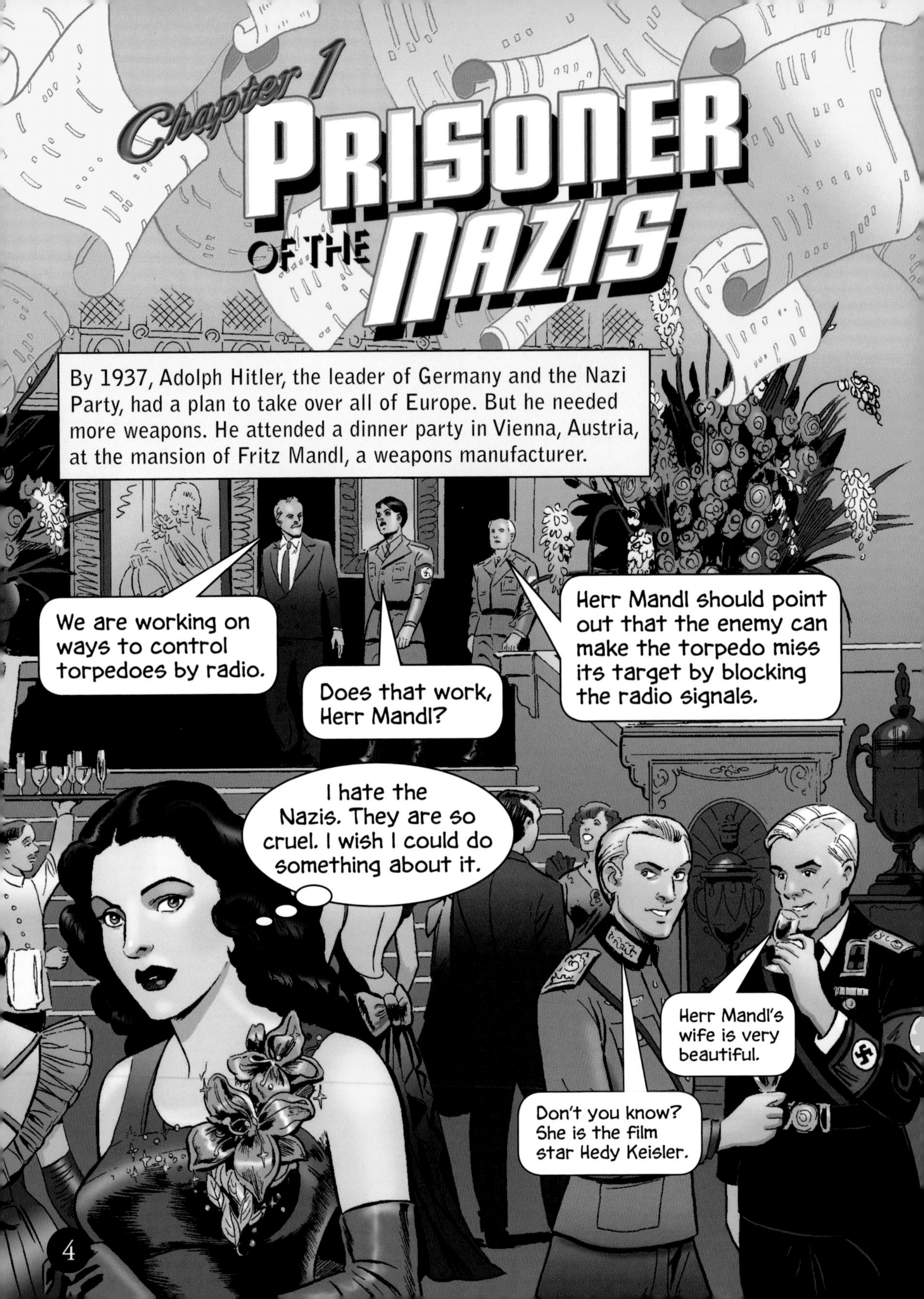
Chapter 1
PRISONER OF THE NAZIS
By 1937, Adolph Hitler, the leader of Germany and the Nazi Party, had a plan to take over all of Europe. But he needed more weapons. He attended a dinner party in Vienna, Austria, at the mansion of Fritz Mandl, a weapons manufacturer.
We are working on ways to control torpedoes by radio.
Does that work, Herr Mandl?
Herr Mandl should point out that the enemy can make the torpedo miss its target by blocking the radio signals.
I hate the Nazis. They are so cruel. I wish I could do something about it.
Herr Mandl's wife is very beautiful.
Don't you know? She is the film star Hedy Keisler.

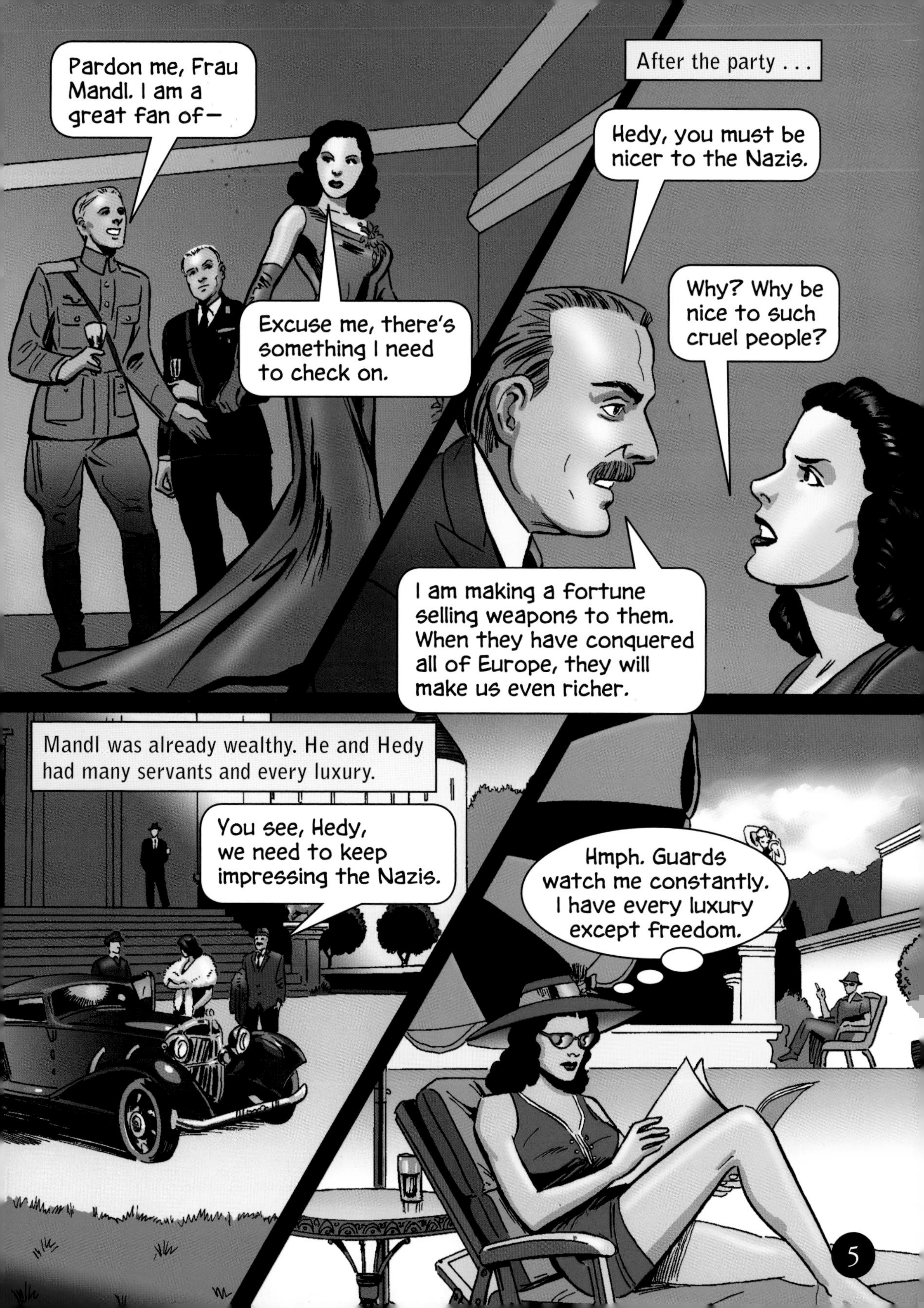
Pardon me, Frau Mandl. I am a great fan of—
Excuse me, there's something I need to check on.
After the party . . .
Hedy, you must be nicer to the Nazis.
Why? Why be nice to such cruel people?
I am making a fortune selling weapons to them. When they have conquered all of Europe, they will make us even richer.
Mandl was already wealthy. He and Hedy had many servants and every luxury.
You see, Hedy, we need to keep impressing the Nazis.
Hmph. Guards watch me constantly. I have every luxury except freedom.

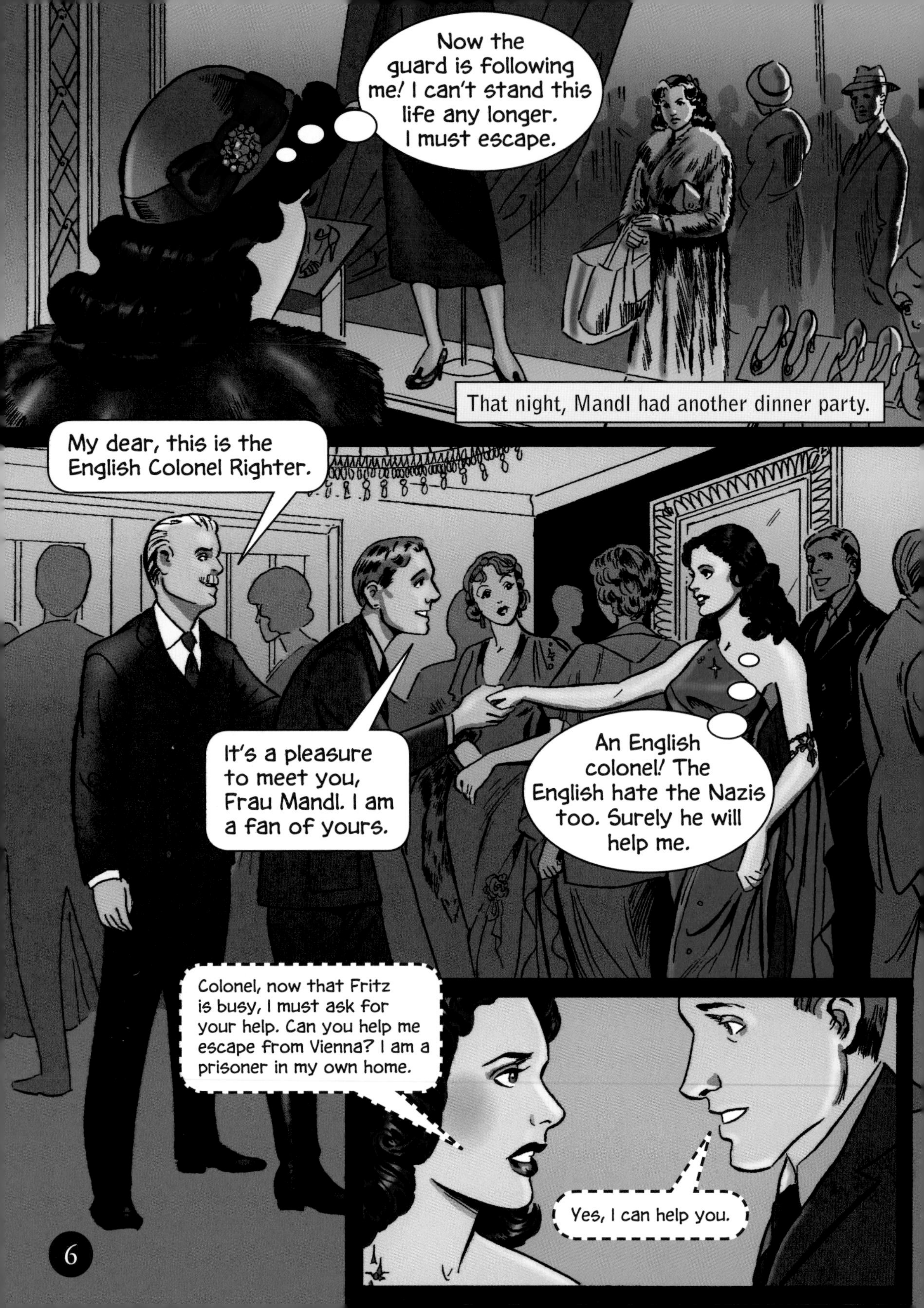
Now the guard is following me! I can't stand this life any longer. I must escape.
That night, Mandl had another dinner party.
My dear, this is the English Colonel Righter.
It's a pleasure to meet you, Frau Mandl. I am a fan of yours.
An English colonel! The English hate the Nazis too. Surely he will help me.
Colonel, now that Fritz is busy, I must ask for your help. Can you help me escape from Vienna? I am a prisoner in my own home.
Yes, I can help you.

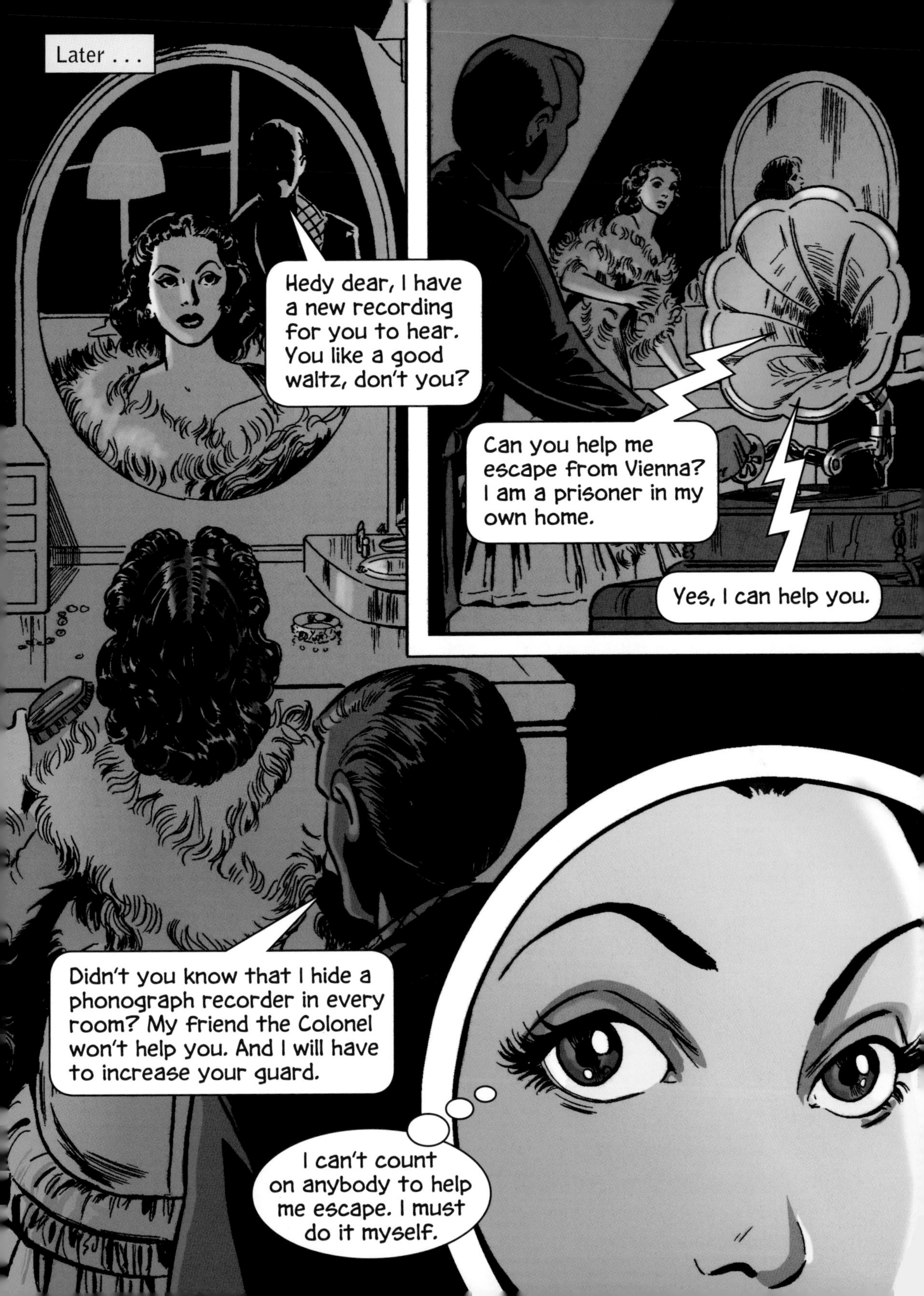

Later . . .
Hedy dear, I have a new recording for you to hear. You like a good waltz, don't you?
Can you help me escape from Vienna? I am a prisoner in my own home.
Yes, I can help you.
Didn't you know that I hide a phonograph recorder in every room? My friend the Colonel won't help you. And I will have to increase your guard.
I can't count on anybody to help me escape. I must do it myself.

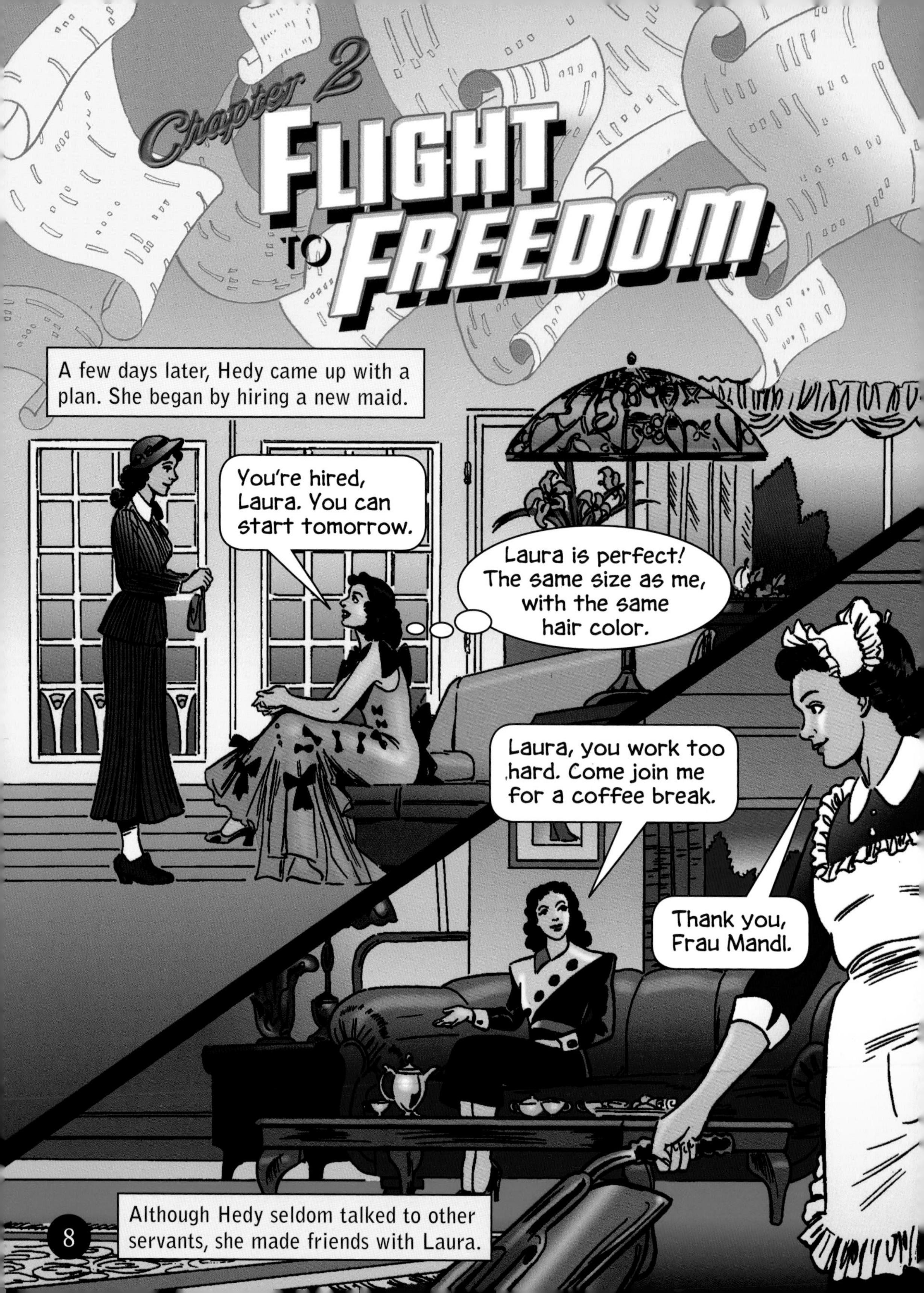
Chapter 2
FLIGHT TO FREEDOM
A few days later, Hedy came up with a plan. She began by hiring a new maid.
You're hired, Laura. You can start tomorrow.
Laura is perfect! The same size as me, with the same hair color.
Laura, you work too hard. Come join me for a coffee break.
Thank you, Frau Mandl.
Although Hedy seldom talked to other servants, she made friends with Laura.

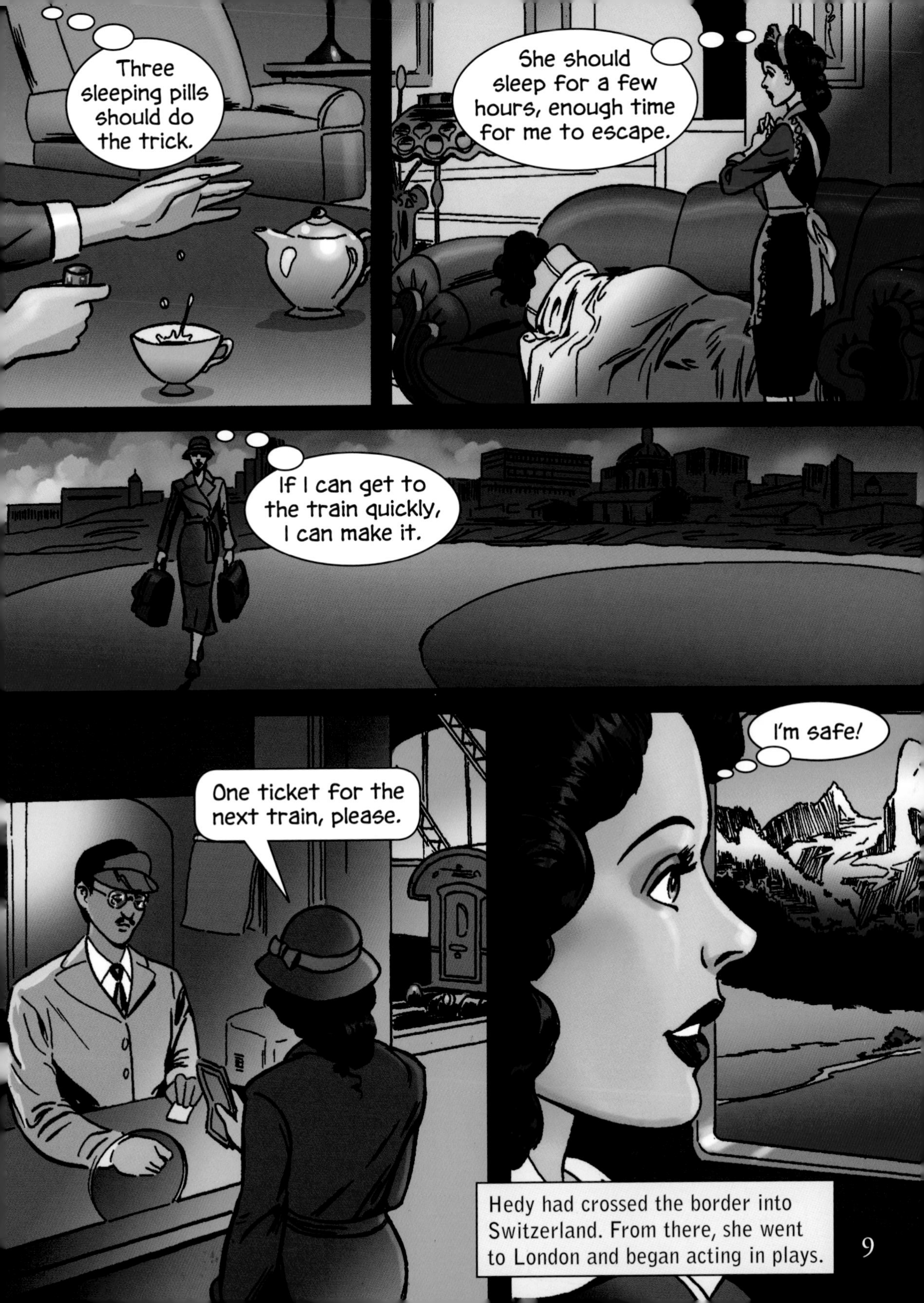
Three sleeping pills should do the trick.
She should sleep for a few hours, enough time for me to escape.
If I can get to the train quickly, I can make it.
One ticket for the next train, please.
I'm safe!
Hedy had crossed the border into Switzerland. From there, she went to London and began acting in plays.

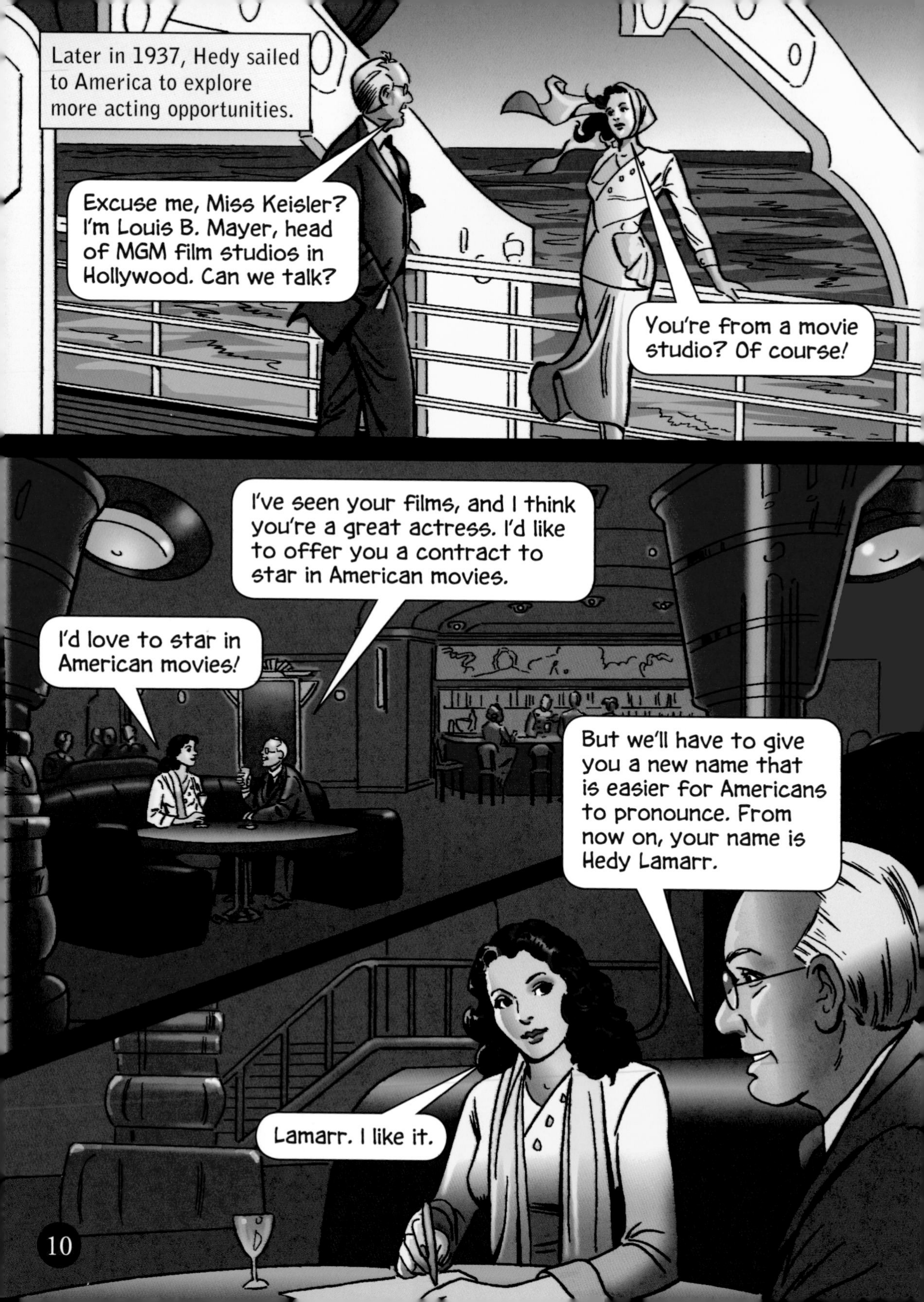
Later in 1937, Hedy sailed to America to explore more acting opportunities.
Excuse me, Miss Keisler? I'm Louis B. Mayer, head of MGM film studios in Hollywood. Can we talk?
You're from a movie studio? Of course!
I've seen your films, and I think you're a great actress. I'd like to offer you a contract to star in American movies.
I'd love to star in American movies!
But we'll have to give you a new name that is easier for Americans to pronounce. From now on, your name is Hedy Lamarr.
Lamarr. I like it.

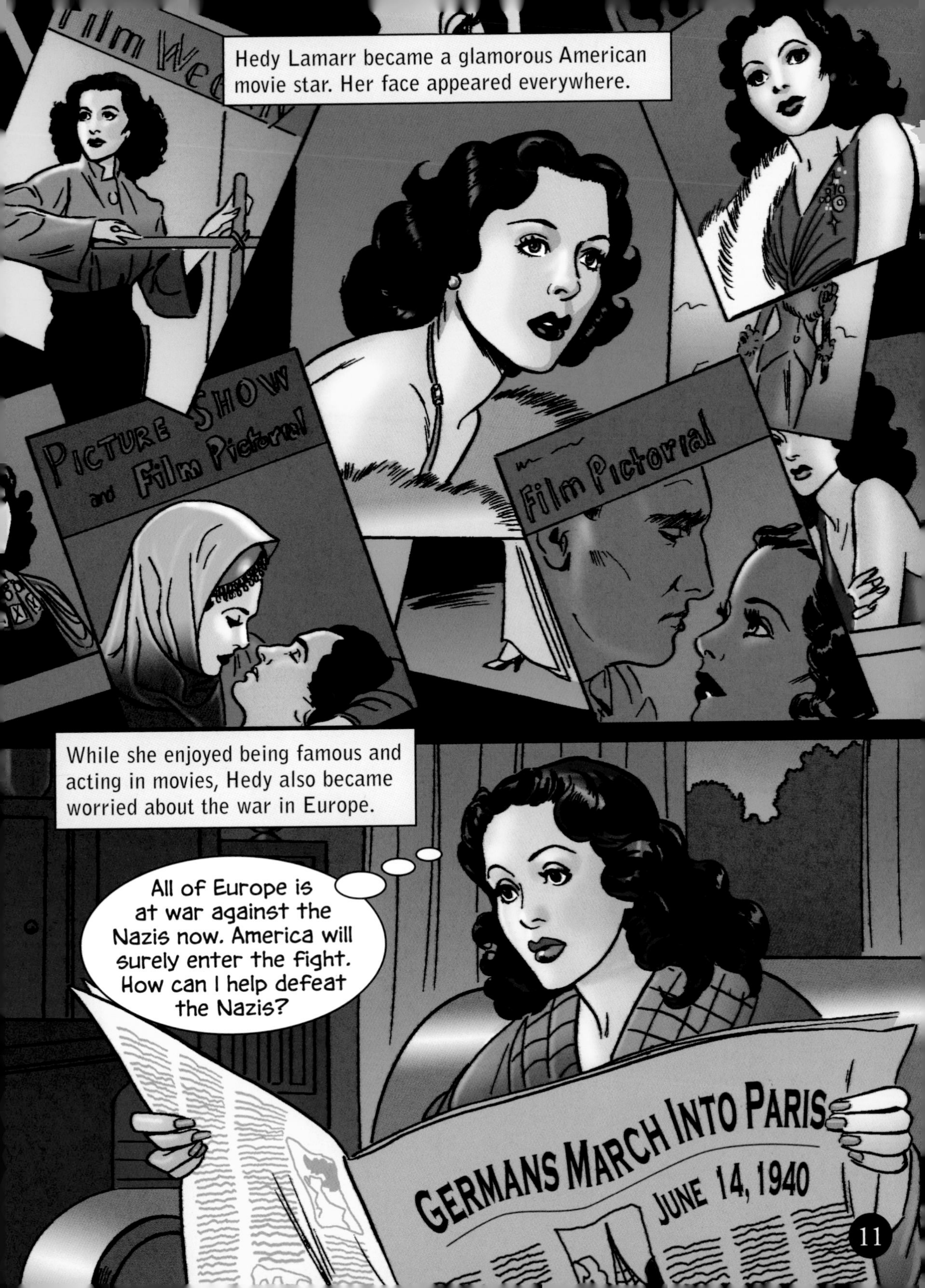

Hedy Lamarr became a glamorous American movie star. Her face appeared everywhere.
Film Weekly
PICTURE SHOW and Film Pictorial
Film Pictorial
While she enjoyed being famous and acting in movies, Hedy also became worried about the war in Europe.
All of Europe is at war against the Nazis now. America will surely enter the fight. How can I help defeat the Nazis?
GERMANS MARCH INTO PARIS
JUNE 14, 1940

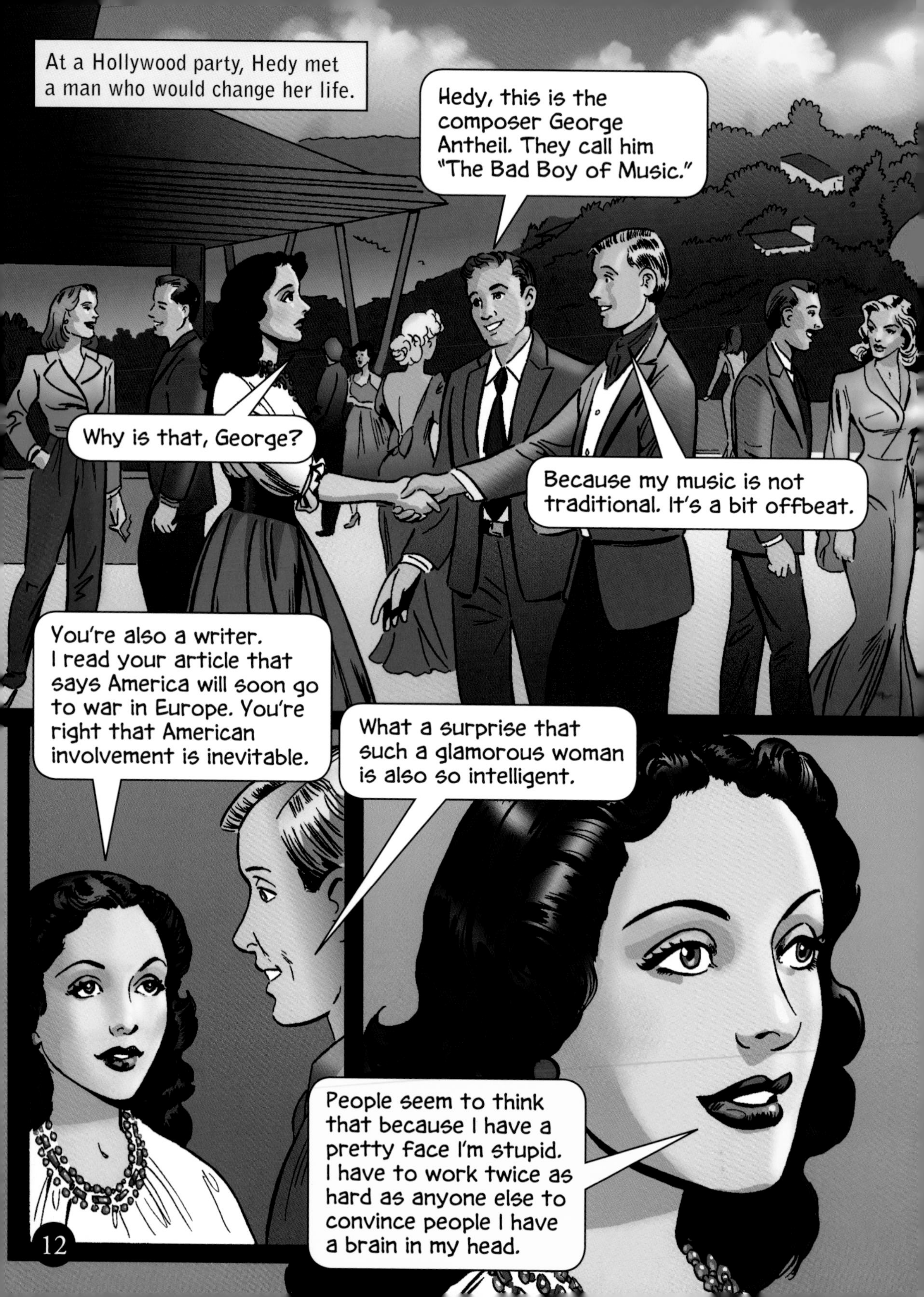
At a Hollywood party, Hedy met a man who would change her life.
Hedy, this is the composer George Antheil. They call him "The Bad Boy of Music."
Why is that, George?
Because my music is not traditional. It's a bit offbeat.
You're also a writer. I read your article that says America will soon go to war in Europe. You're right that American involvement is inevitable.
What a surprise that such a glamorous woman is also so intelligent.
People seem to think that because I have a pretty face I'm stupid. I have to work twice as hard as anyone else to convince people I have a brain in my head.

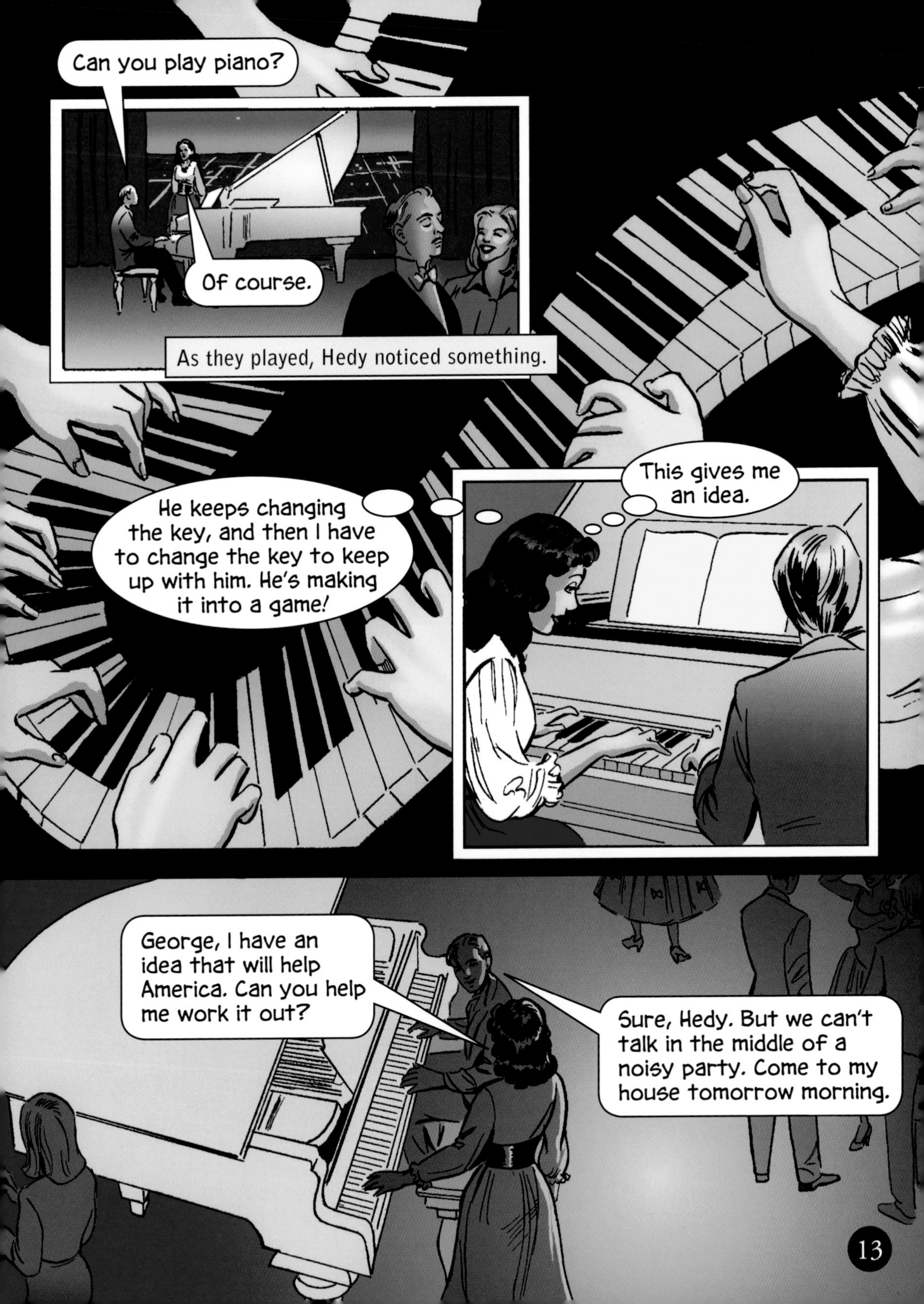

Can you play piano?
Of course.
As they played, Hedy noticed something.
He keeps changing the key, and then I have to change the key to keep up with him. He's making it into a game!
This gives me an idea.
George, I have an idea that will help America. Can you help me work it out?
Sure, Hedy. But we can't talk in the middle of a noisy party. Come to my house tomorrow morning.

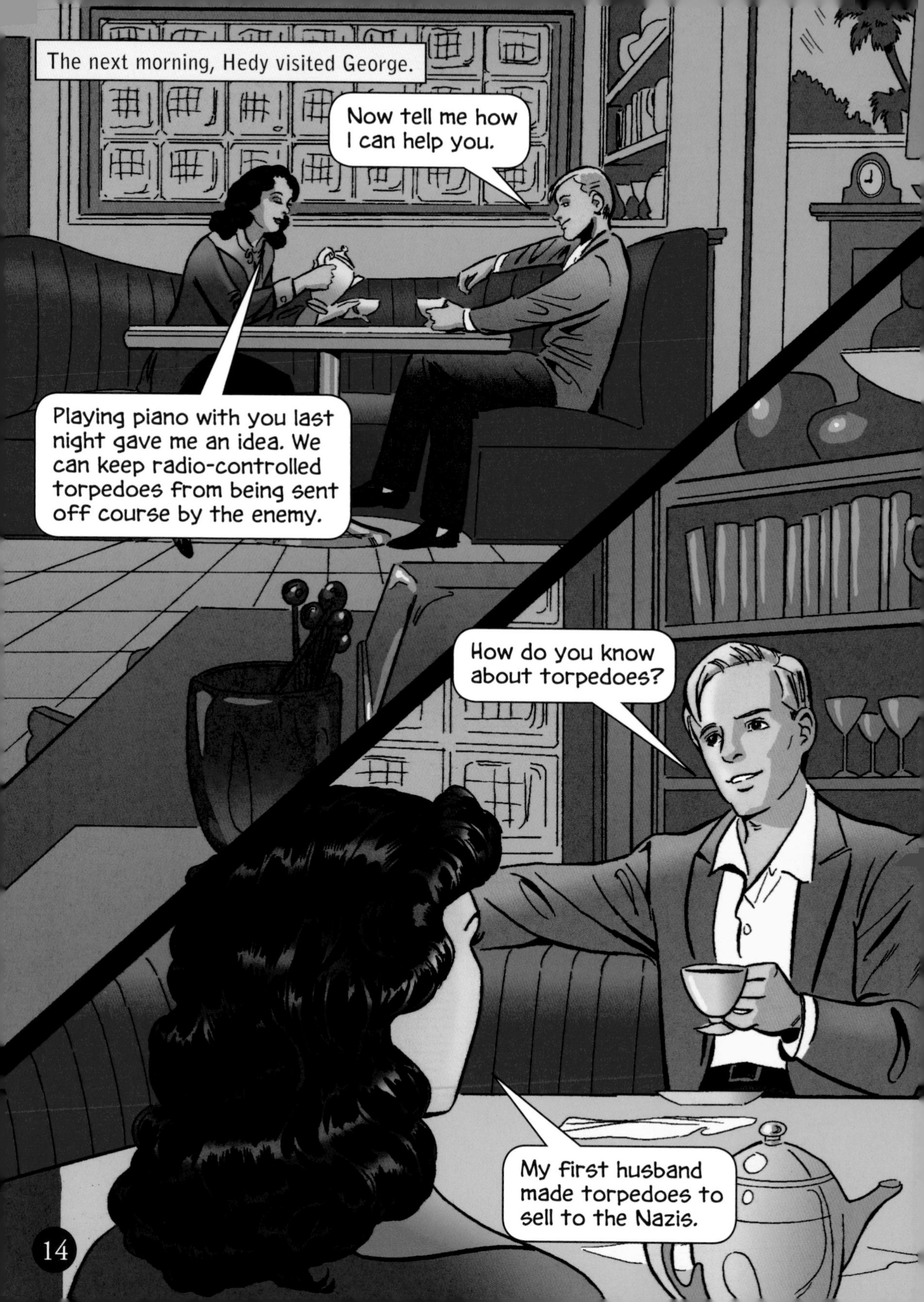
The next morning, Hedy visited George.
Now tell me how I can help you.
Playing piano with you last night gave me an idea. We can keep radio-controlled torpedoes from being sent off course by the enemy.
How do you know about torpedoes?
My first husband made torpedoes to sell to the Nazis.

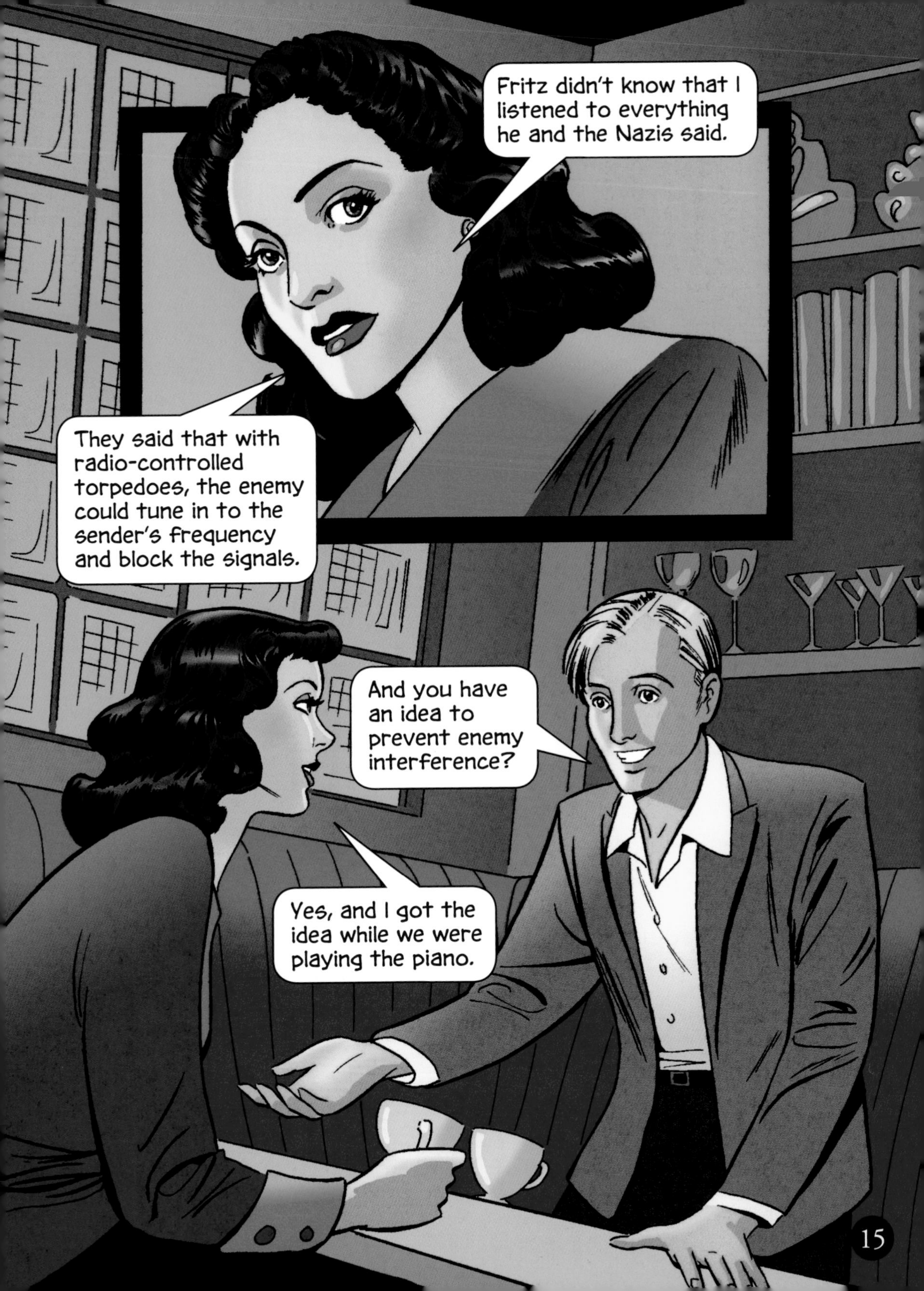
Fritz didn't know that I listened to everything he and the Nazis said.
They said that with radio-controlled torpedoes, the enemy could tune in to the sender's frequency and block the signals.
And you have an idea to prevent enemy interference?
Yes, and I got the idea while we were playing the piano.

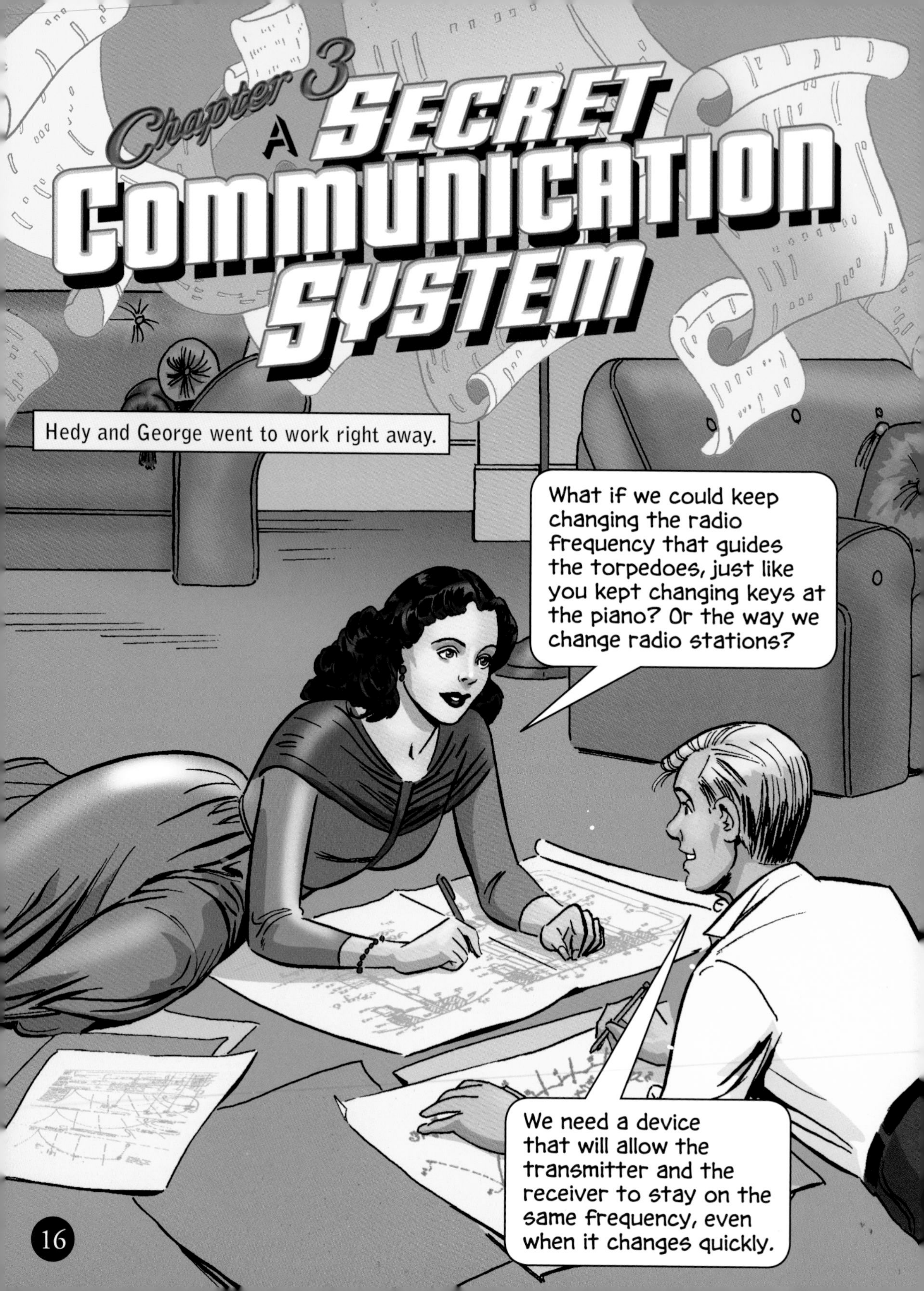
Chapter 3
A SECRET COMMUNICATION SYSTEM
Hedy and George went to work right away.
What if we could keep changing the radio frequency that guides the torpedoes, just like you kept changing keys at the piano? Or the way we change radio stations?
We need a device that will allow the transmitter and the receiver to stay on the same frequency, even when it changes quickly.

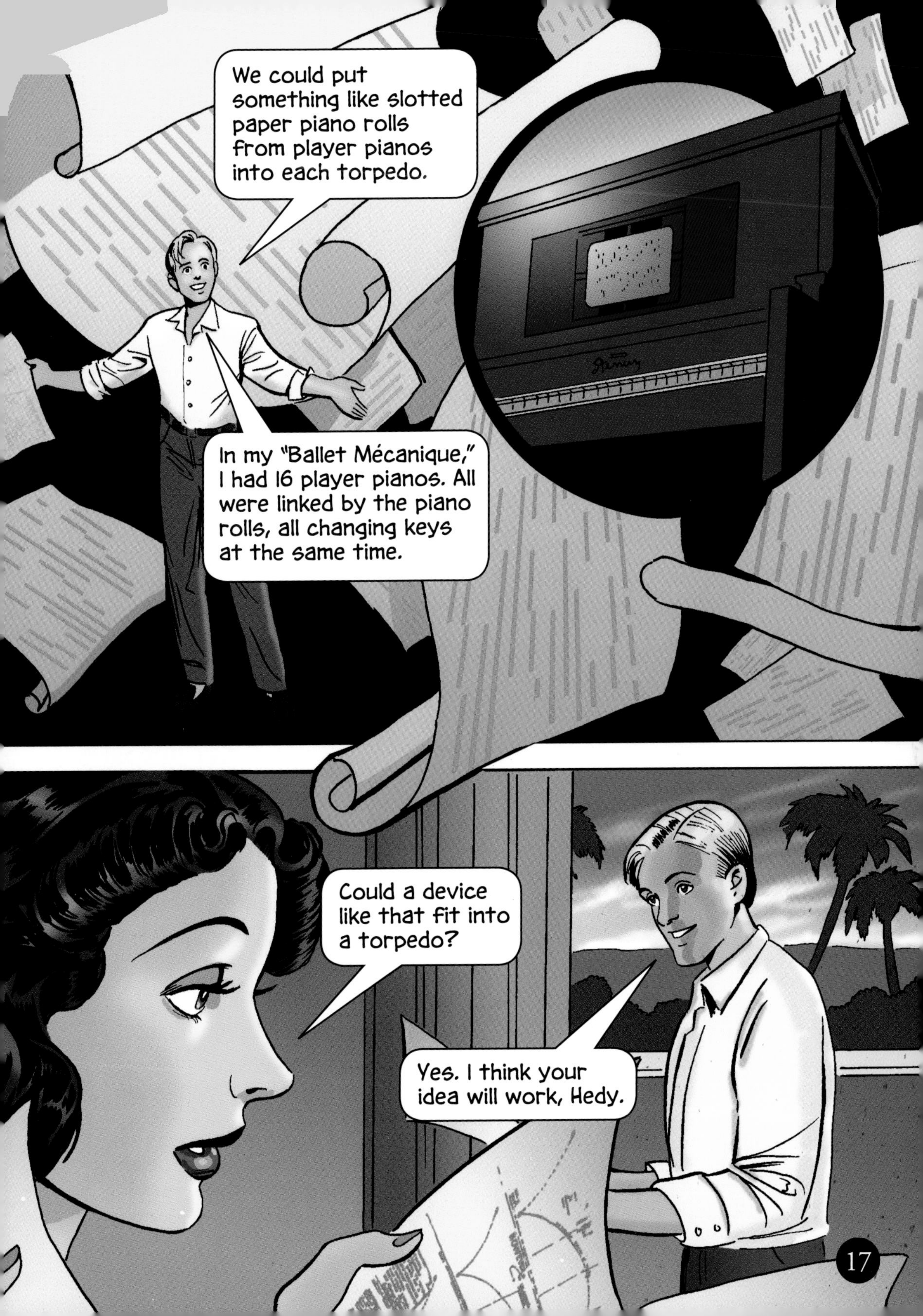
We could put something like slotted paper piano rolls from player pianos into each torpedo.
In my "Ballet Mécanique," I had 16 player pianos. All were linked by the piano rolls, all changing keys at the same time.
Could a device like that fit into a torpedo?
Yes. I think your idea will work, Hedy.

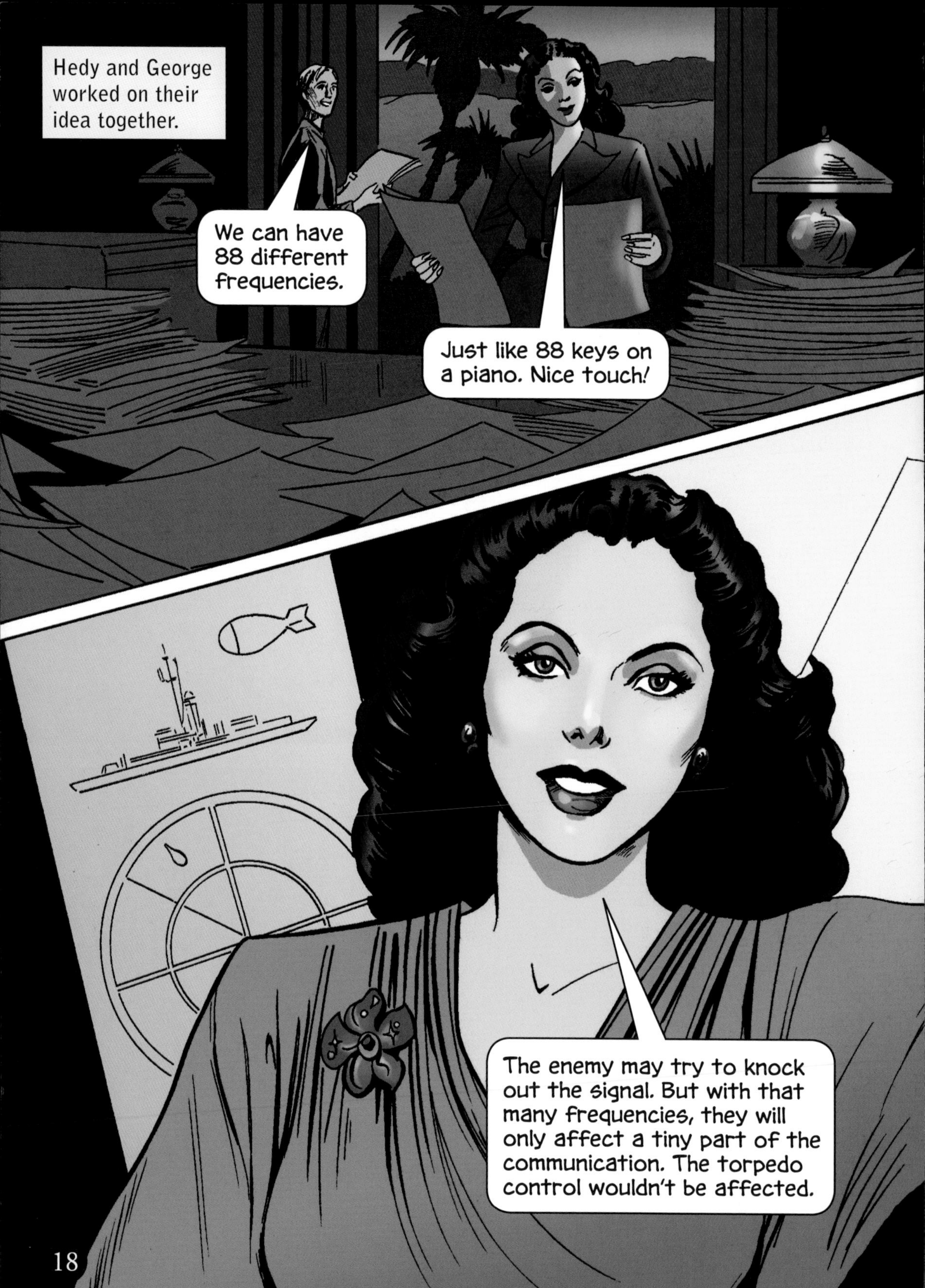
Hedy and George worked on their idea together.
We can have 88 different frequencies.
Just like 88 keys on a piano. Nice touch!
The enemy may try to knock out the signal. But with that many frequencies, they will only affect a tiny part of the communication. The torpedo control wouldn't be affected.

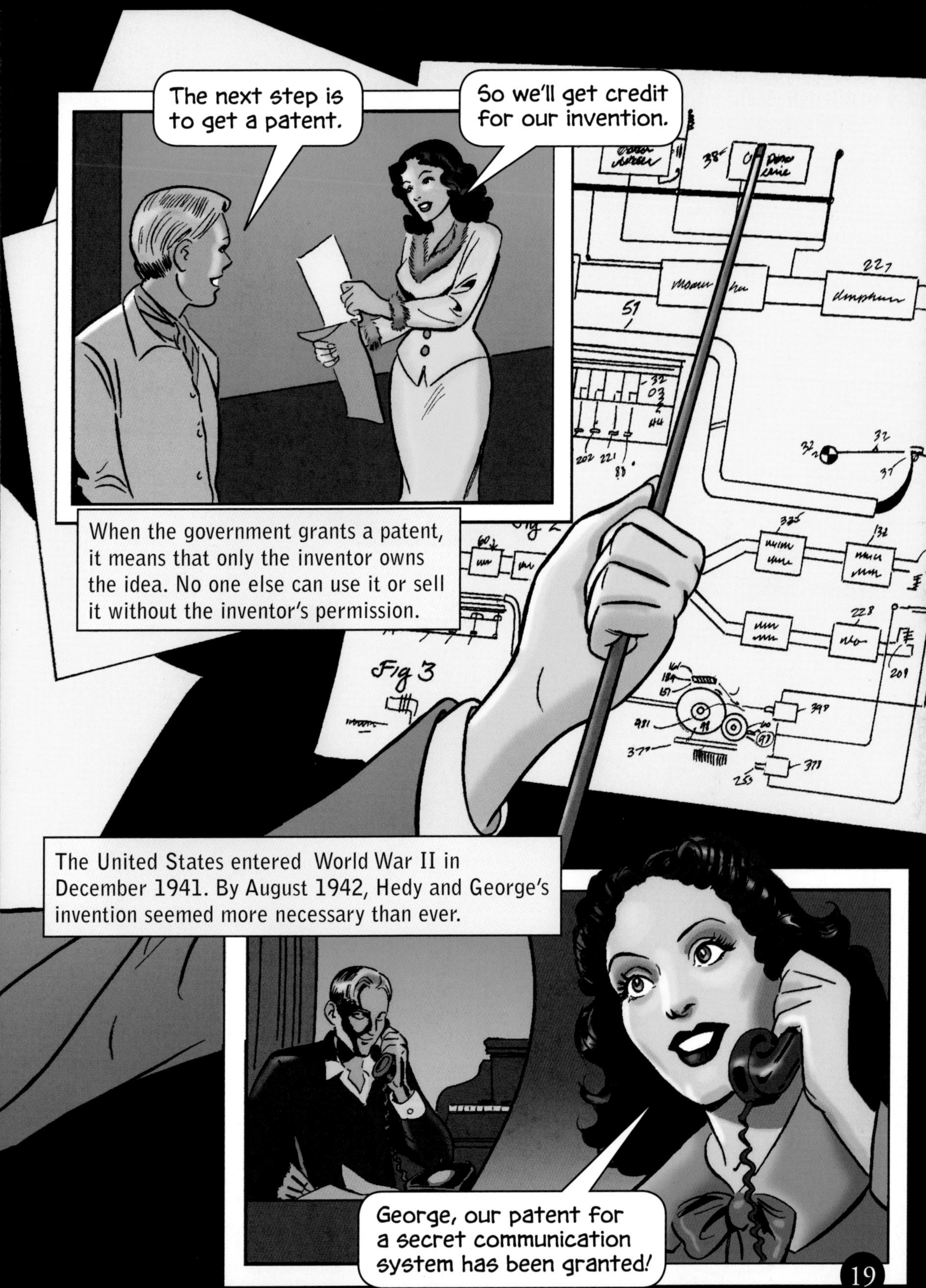
The next step is to get a patent.
So we'll get credit for our invention.
When the government grants a patent, it means that only the inventor owns the idea. No one else can use it or sell it without the inventor's permission.
The United States entered World War II in December 1941. By August 1942, Hedy and George's invention seemed more necessary than ever.
George, our patent for a secret communication system has been granted!

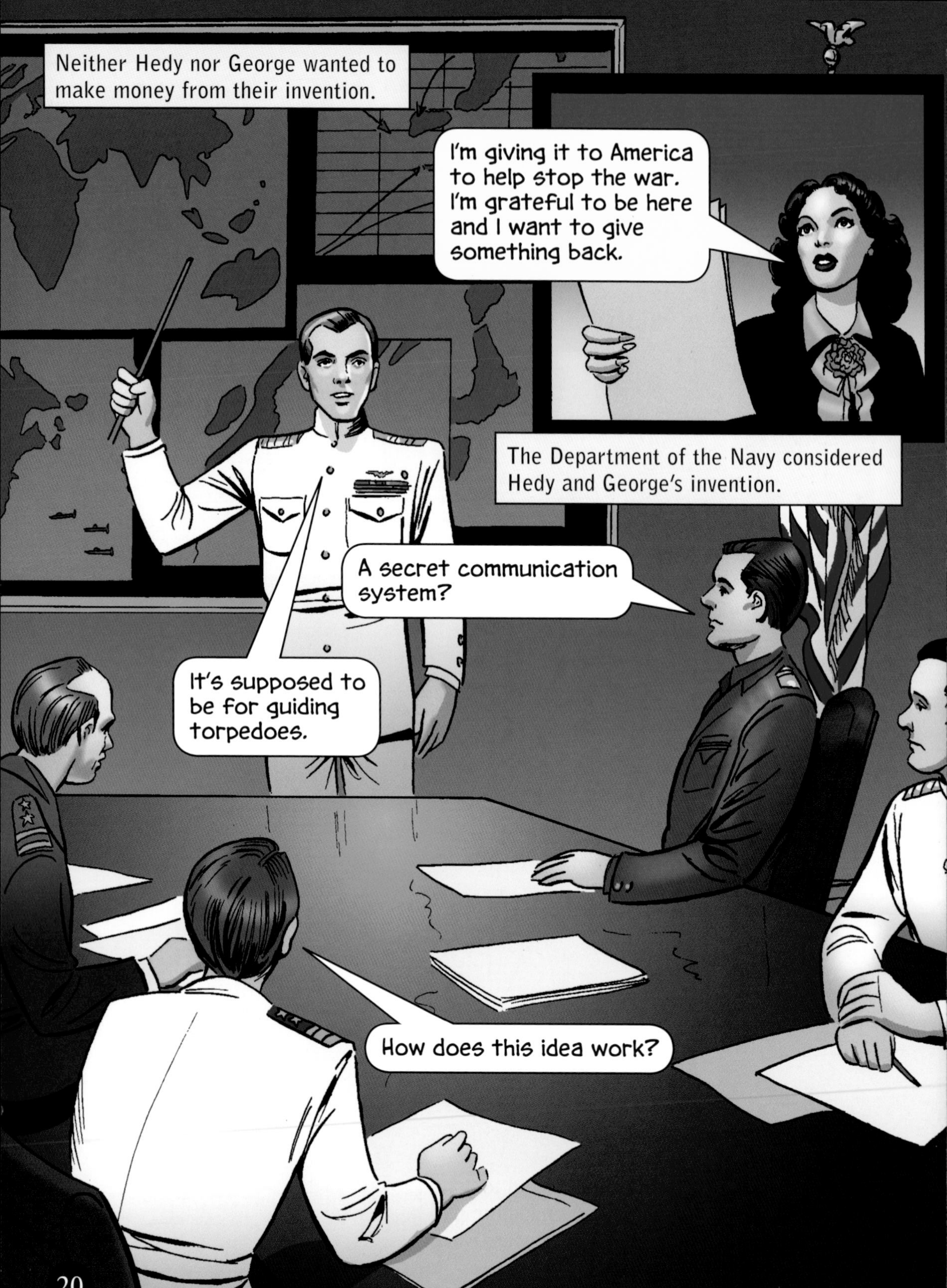
Neither Hedy nor George wanted to make money from their invention.
I'm giving it to America to help stop the war. I'm grateful to be here and I want to give something back.
The Department of the Navy considered Hedy and George's invention.
A secret communication system?
It's supposed to be for guiding torpedoes.
How does this idea work?

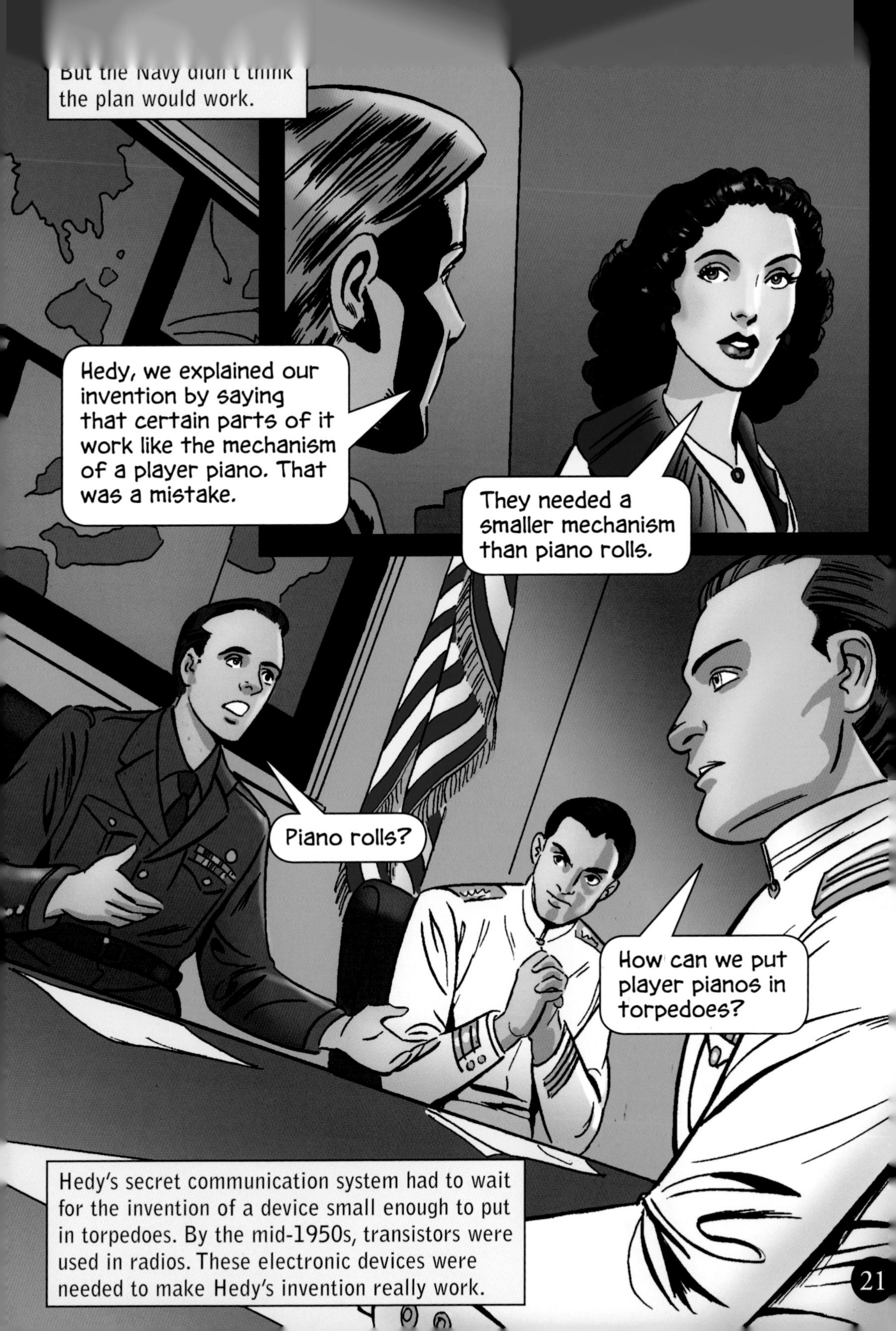
But the Navy didn't think the plan would work.
Hedy, we explained our invention by saying that certain parts of it work like the mechanism of a player piano. That was a mistake.
They needed a smaller mechanism than piano rolls.
Piano rolls?
How can we put player pianos in torpedoes?
Hedy's secret communication system had to wait for the invention of a device small enough to put in torpedoes. By the mid-1950s, transistors were used in radios. These electronic devices were needed to make Hedy's invention really work.

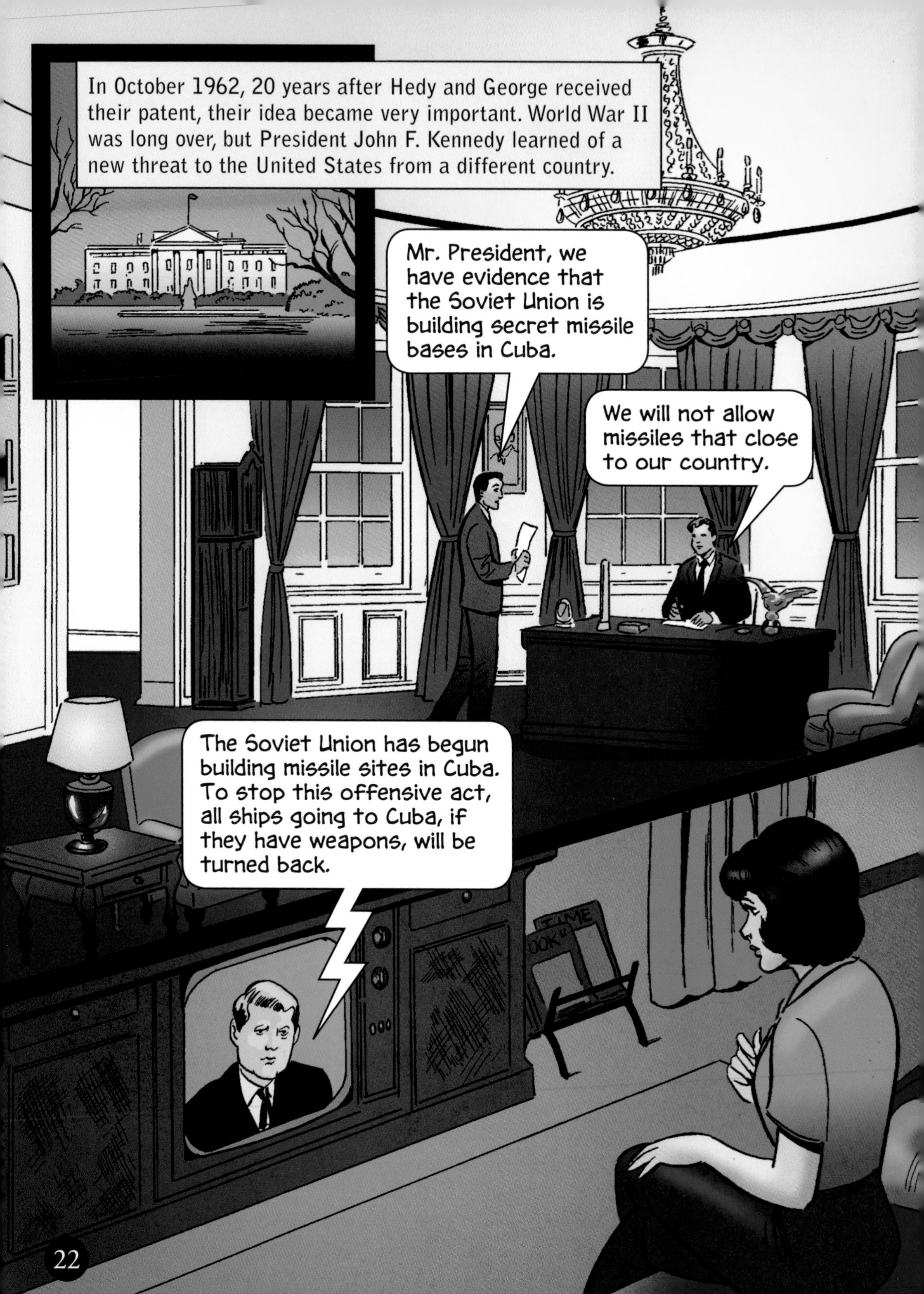

In October 1962, 20 years after Hedy and George received their patent, their idea became very important. World War II was long over, but President John F. Kennedy learned of a new threat to the United States from a different country.
Mr. President, we have evidence that the Soviet Union is building secret missile bases in Cuba.
We will not allow missiles that close to our country.
The Soviet Union has begun building missile sites in Cuba. To stop this offensive act, all ships going to Cuba, if they have weapons, will be turned back.

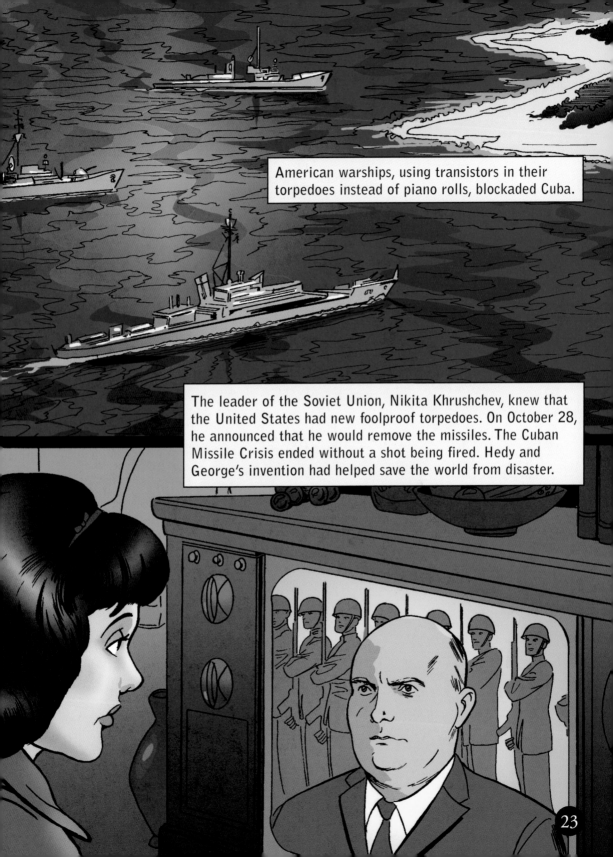

American warships, using transistors in their torpedoes instead of piano rolls, blockaded Cuba.

The leader of the Soviet Union, Nikita Khrushchev, knew that the United States had new foolproof torpedoes. On October 28, he announced that he would remove the missiles. The Cuban Missile Crisis ended without a shot being fired. Hedy and George's invention had helped save the world from disaster.

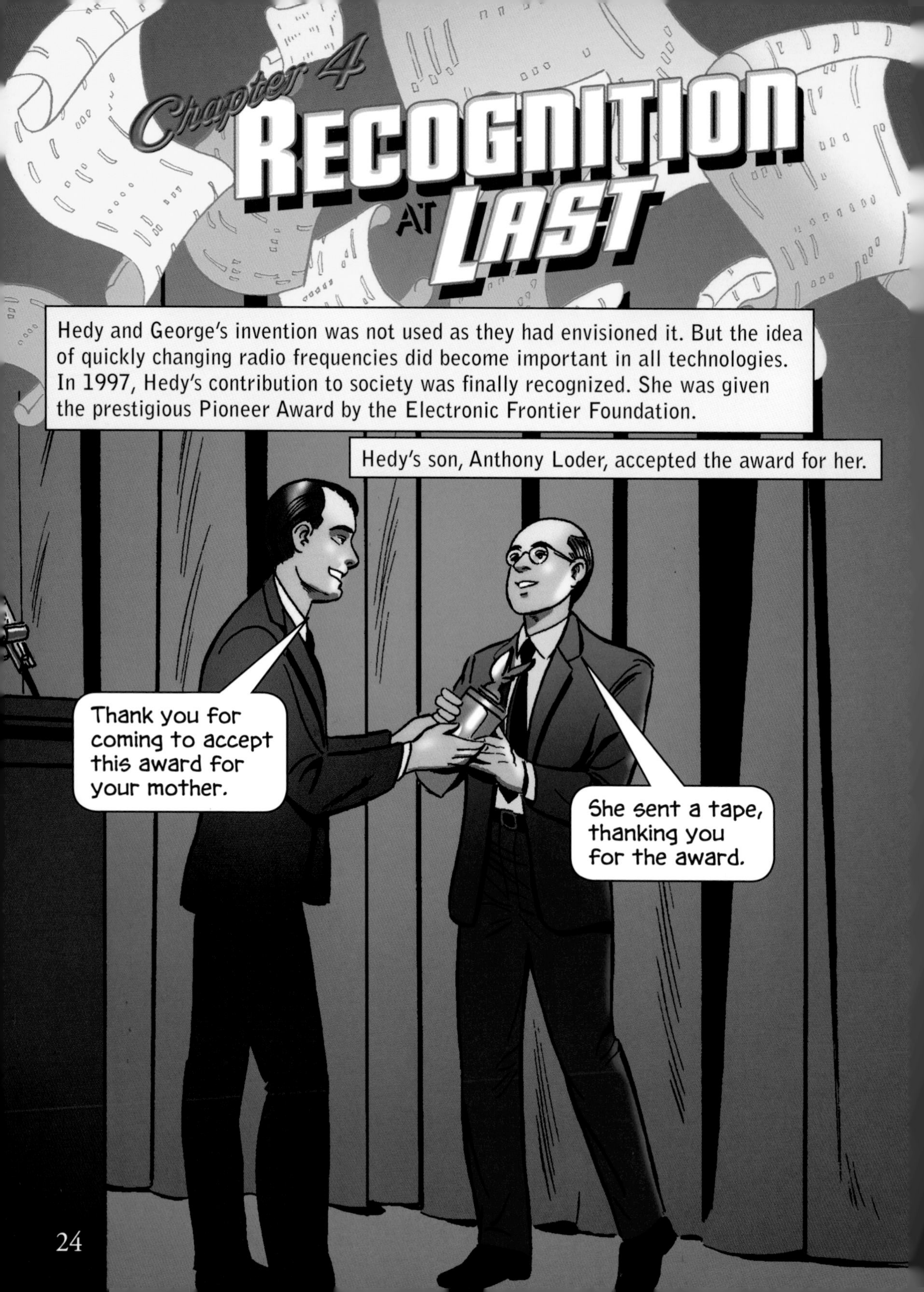
Chapter 4
RECOGNITION AT LAST
Hedy and George's invention was not used as they had envisioned it. But the idea of quickly changing radio frequencies did become important in all technologies. In 1997, Hedy's contribution to society was finally recognized. She was given the prestigious Pioneer Award by the Electronic Frontier Foundation.
Hedy's son, Anthony Loder, accepted the award for her.
Thank you for coming to accept this award for your mother.
She sent a tape, thanking you for the award.

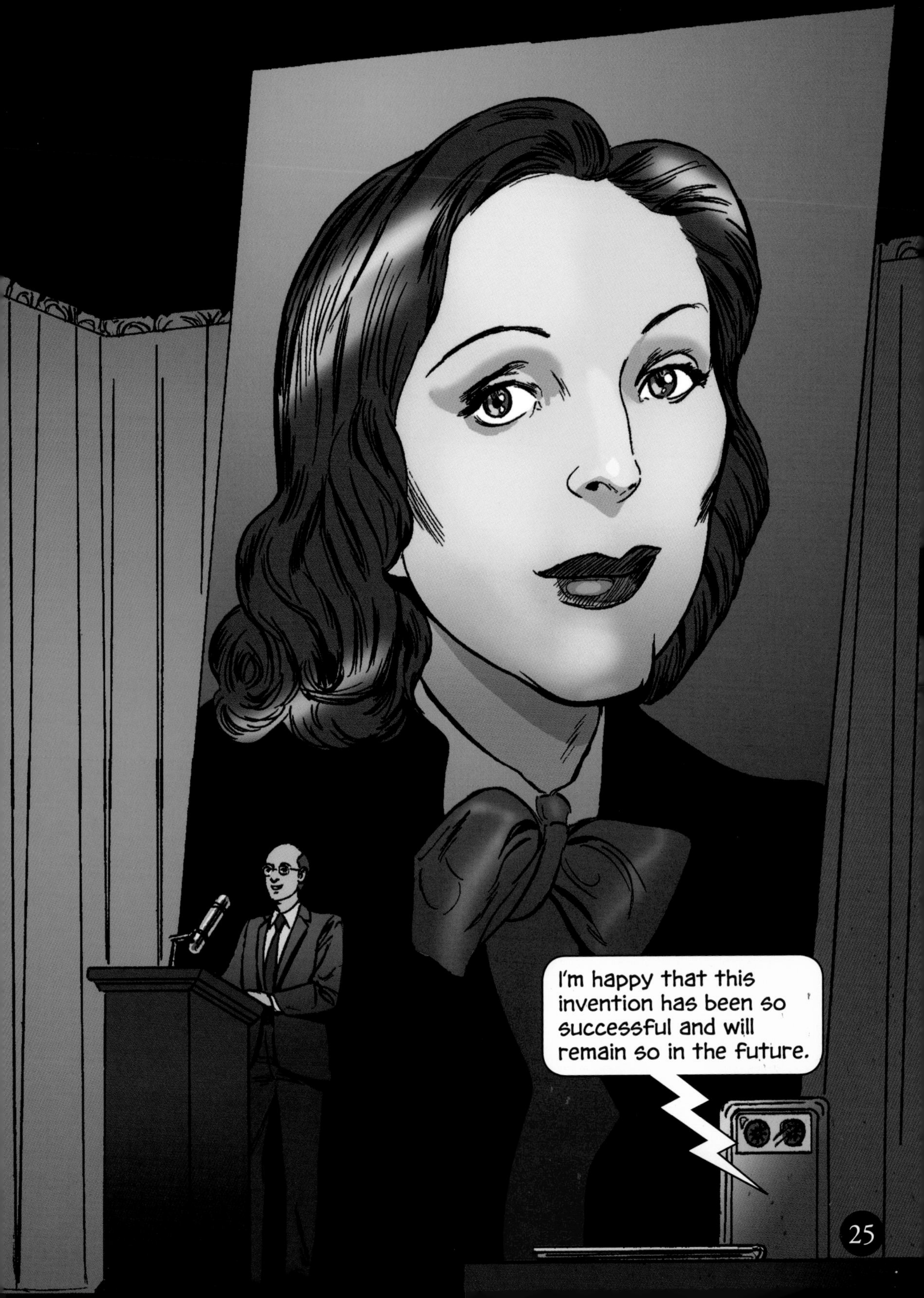
I'm happy that this invention has been so successful and will remain so in the future.

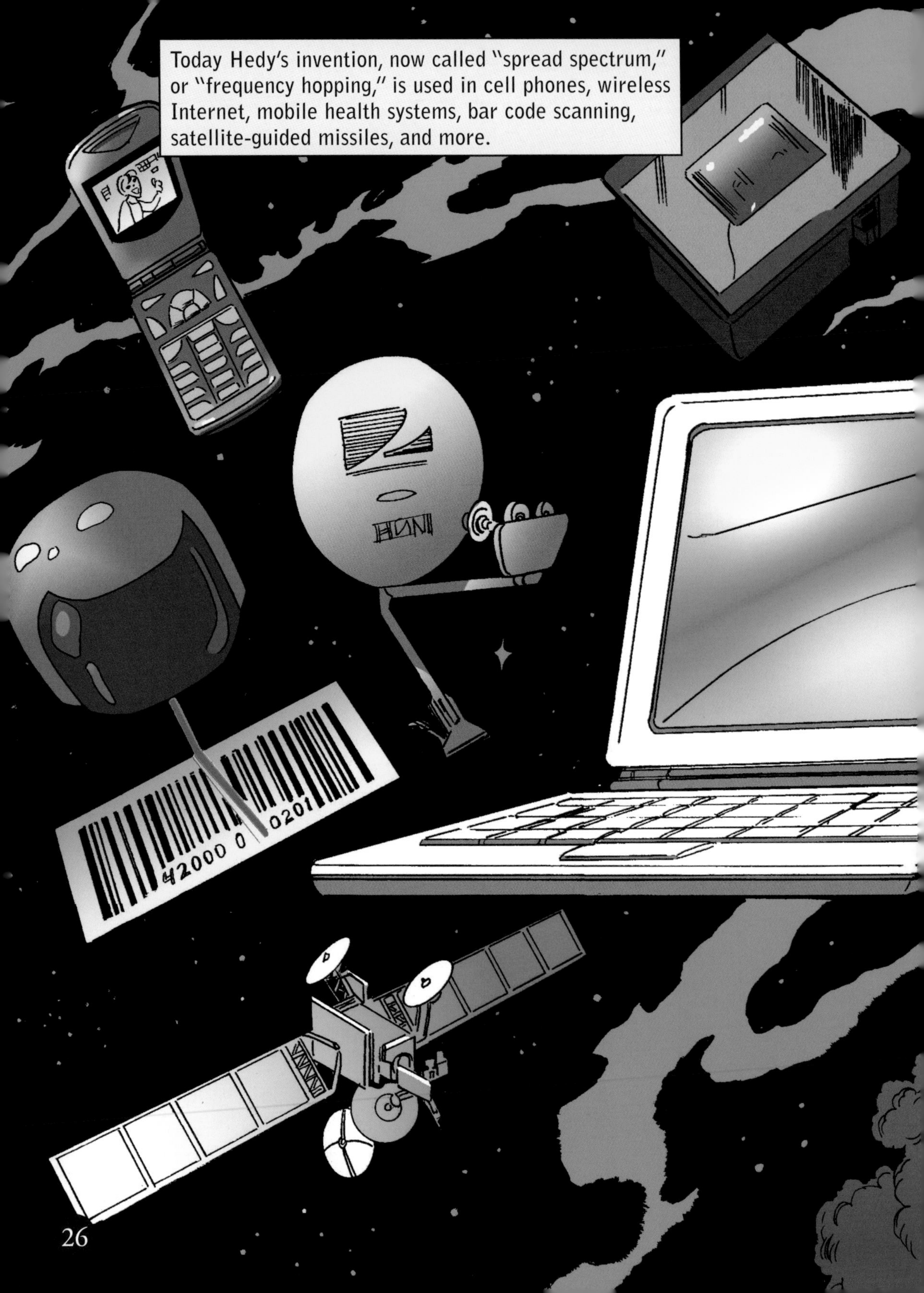
Today Hedy's invention, now called "spread spectrum," or "frequency hopping," is used in cell phones, wireless Internet, mobile health systems, bar code scanning, satellite-guided missiles, and more.
42000 0
0201

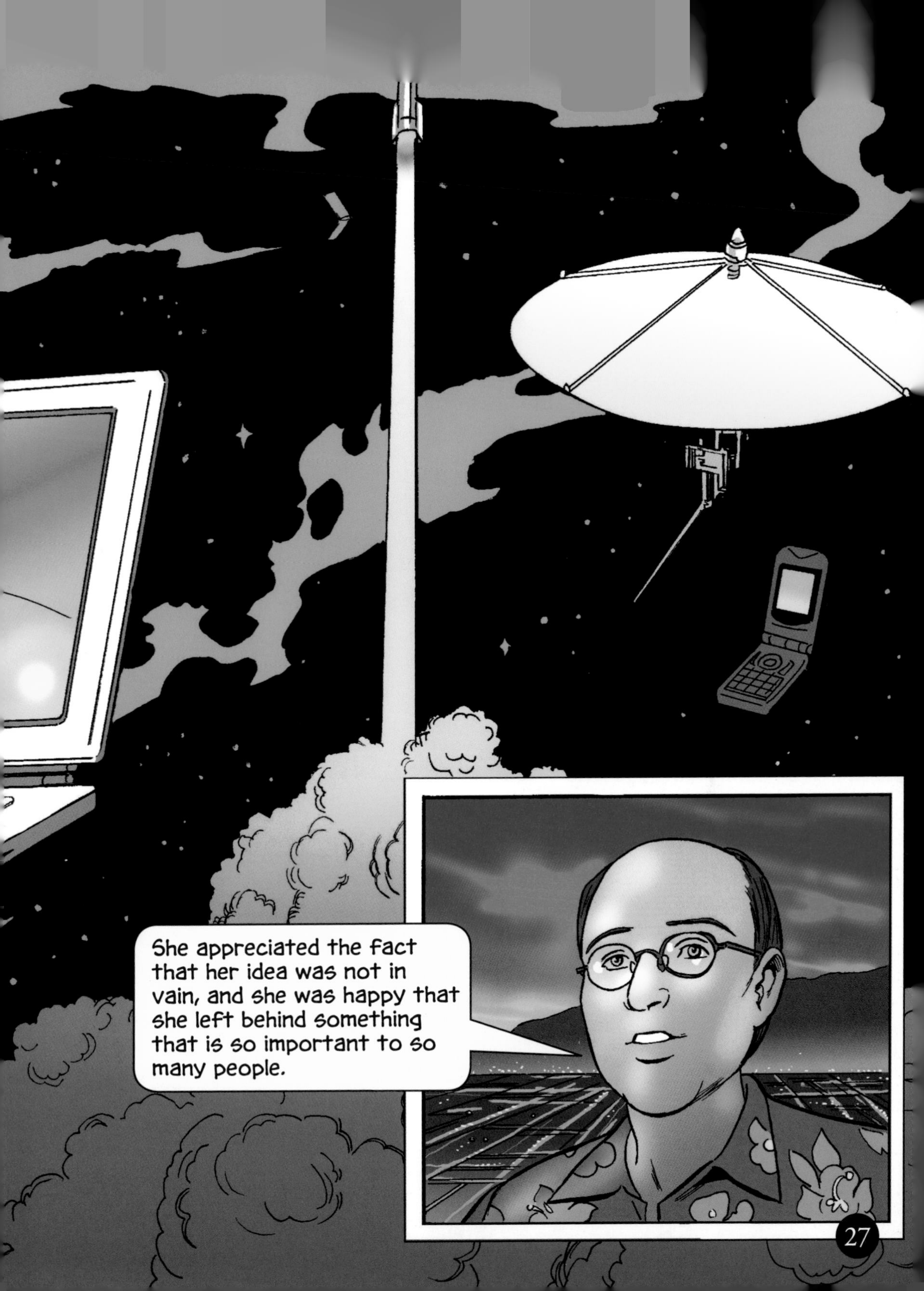
She appreciated the fact that her idea was not in vain, and she was happy that she left behind something that is so important to so many people.

More about HEDY LAMARR AND HER INVENTION

- Hedy Lamarr, as Hedwig Keisler, made her first movie at the age of 17.

- Hedy Lamarr was married and divorced six times, to Fritz Mandl, Gene Markey, John Loder, Ted Stauffer, W. Howard Lee, and Lewis J. Boles. Her patent is credited to H. K. Markey (Hedwig Keisler Markey), because at the time she was married to Gene Markey.

- During World War II, Hedy sold 7 million dollars worth of war bonds in a single evening. The U.S. government sold war bonds to help fund the war.

- Hedy's son, Anthony Loder, owns a phone store, selling products that were made possible by his mother's invention.

- George Antheil died in 1959, before he could see the invention used at all.

- Hedy was born November 9, 1914, and she died on January 19, 2000.

About Player Pianos

Player pianos were popular during the late 1800s and early 1900s. These pianos played without anyone pressing the keys. Instead, the keys moved by a mechanical system that used piano rolls. A paper piano roll had holes punched in it. The position and length of the punched holes determined the notes played on the piano.

Who Were the Nazis?

The Nazis were led by Adolph Hitler. They invaded and conquered most of Europe. In 1939, Hitler and the Nazis invaded Poland. England, which had signed a treaty to come to Poland's defense, declared war on Nazi Germany. World War II had begun. From 1940 to 1941, the Nazis bombed London night and day, killing thousands of British people. After Japan attacked Pearl Harbor, Hawaii, in 1941, the United States entered the war. After four more years of fighting, World War II finally ended in 1945, with the defeat of Germany and its allies, Italy and Japan.

GLOSSARY

blockade (blok-ADE)—to close off an area to keep ships from going in or out

frequency (FREE-kwuhn-see)—the number of cycles per second of a radio wave; radio stations use different frequencies.

interference (in-tur-FIHR-uhnss)—something that interrupts a radio signal so that it cannot be read or heard

mechanism (MEK-uh-niz-uhm)—a system of moving parts inside a machine

receiver (ri-SEE-vur)—a device that receives radio signals and turns them into sound or pictures

torpedo (tor-PEE-doh)—an underwater missile that explodes when it hits a target, such as a ship

transistor (tran-ZISS-tur)—a small electronic device that controls the flow of electric current

transmitter (TRANS-mit-ur)—a device that sends out radio signals

INTERNET SITES

FactHound offers a safe, fun way to find Internet sites related to this book. All of the sites on FactHound have been researched by our staff.

Here's how:

1. Visit *www.facthound.com*
2. Choose your grade level.
3. Type in this book ID **0736864792** for age-appropriate sites. You may also browse subjects by clicking on letters, or by clicking on pictures and words.
4. Click on the **Fetch It** button.

FactHound will fetch the best sites for you!

READ MORE

Chrisp, Peter. *The Cuban Missile Crisis.* The Cold War. Milwaukee: World Almanac Library, 2002.

Goldstein, Margaret J. *World War II. Europe.* Chronicle of America's Wars. Minneapolis: Lerner, 2004.

Mattern, Joanne. *From Radio to the Wireless Web.* Transportation and Communication. Berkeley Heights, N.J.: Enslow, 2002.

BIBLIOGRAPHY

Braun, Hans-Joachim. "Advanced Weaponry of the Stars." *American Heritage of Invention & Technology.* Spring 1997.

Hover, Helen. "Popping Questions at Hedy Lamarr." *Motion Picture.* March 1945.

Loder, Anthony. E-mail interview with the author, May 2005.

Skolsky, Sidney. "Handbook on Hedy." *Photoplay.* May 1944.

INDEX